#Thriving20s

K. Franco

ISBN:0692758038
ISBN-978-0-692-75803-8

CREATIVE MILLENNIAL

May you find yourself in this thing, we call life.

May you develop mastery even in chaos.

Life has a way of teaching us powerful lessons.

We as students have a duty to remain aware,

patient, and humble.

May you live your most thrilling, and unimaginable dreams.

May you continue to climb to the highest ladders of this universe.

Even when you've exhausted your final breath.

May you always grasp the key of growth.

Be a light to others oppose to rainy storms.

Lastly millennial may you paint your love,

in every crevice of this mystic world.

-K. Franco

TABLE OF CONTENTS

Introduction

This book was born after a night of hanging out with

my eccentric friend Nic. She had pulled out her MacBook

containing hundreds of pictures. Seriously: hundreds. I

didn't know you could store so much data on an Apple

product! There was an abundance of pictures of us

throughout the last few years. There were photos of us

traveling to exciting cities and countries, such as Las Vegas,

New York City, Greece, and Peru. There were pictures of us

at parties, music festivals, and skydiving. I mean, the variety

of photos she had saved was endless. Viewing all of them

transported me to those different times in my life, and it put a smile on my face.

There was a common denominator in all these photos: it appeared like I was having the time of my life. It was evident by the photos that I was having a blast. I was laughing, smiling, dancing, and while some of them were kind of embarrassing, even those were worth a really good laugh. I began to reflect on where I was during those periods of my life. Although now I know I was having the time of my life, at the time I thought life was so hard. I would complain about how lost in life I was, and how challenging adulthood appear to be. I recall complaining about the relationships I embarked on, how difficult school was, how stressful my job was, and just about anything else I could.

I came to the realization that I had not fully savored every moment in my life. My perspective was so skewed.

How wrong was I to view life in such troubling way? Now I am certain that my life has been filled with a lot of joy, thrilling experiences, life lessons, and growth. At the time I believed that I had only a few good moments and the rest were mediocre. That wasn't the case. The truth is that I have had a very flavorful life and I continue to do so. I've been granted the opportunity, to grow, to learn, to impact, and to experience true happiness. I've realized that every situation that probably didn't make much sense to me at the time has shaped my life into what it is today. I've met meaningful people throughout this journey; some have stayed, others have left. I've come certain that one event leads you to another. I learned that it's important to be flexible and to go with the flow of life.

The lifesaver was learning when to let go of situations that no longer served a purpose in my life. I opened myself up to live life freely. I started discovering who I was. I traveled and went on exciting adventures. I even moved to sultry and sizzling Miami. Taking the leap and moving to Miami allowed me to grow as a young adult making my way into adulthood. I'm blessed to be writing this book, in such a beautiful, vibrant city, which I fall more in love with everyday.

Another major factor that influenced this book was that I know as a 20-something year old I need all the help I can get in "adulting", I can assume the same for the remaining of 20 year olds running around with their heads chopped off. Unfortunately, we don't really don't have a manual for Adulthood-101. We can't just open it up and follow certain steps to lead us to be the cookie-cutter adult. At times the informal information we do get can be overwhelming. We are flooded with so much information on how to how we should be dating, eating, and just plain living. We are given advice from our guardians, mentors, teachers, friends, hell, even social media. Who do we listen to?

I used to be that kid who would admire adults and say "One day, I'll have all the answers. I will have life figured out, and I will be able to do whatever I want." How gullible was I? I learned the hard way that there's no magical transformation that occurs when you become a legal adult. There's no one moment where you just wake up and have it all together. The easiest way to live a fulfilling life is to enjoy the whole process.

What also drove me to put all my words on to paper was due to my work in the public sector. I work as a problem-solver for the members of the community who have been through unfortunate circumstances. I help them transform their lives. What I do for a living is beyond just a nine-to-five. I'm at service to those who have lost all hope in humanity, included sometimes themselves. I instill hope in others to allow them to take the proper steps to self-sufficiency and a brighter outlook for their future. Coming with my experience helping people, I have taken the lead on mentoring the at-risk youth. The youth are always asking questions: "What does it mean to be a grown-up?" "How do you know if you are making the right choices?" "What if you make a poor decision?"

So I compiled all of my experiences, the books I've read, and advice from mentors and other individuals who have discovered their paths to happiness. In reality, life is amazing, everything ends up falling into place, and each experience connects and helps you to the following one. Meanwhile, there are many things we might exhaust our energy on that actually don't matter.

This book will give you the seven game changers on how to smoothly transition into your thriving 20s. It will also help you make sure that you are really celebrating your journey to the fullest. We only have one chance on making this thing we call life count. There is a reason why you have been given this opportunity, so always keep that in mind.

Chapter 1

TAKE A BREATHER

How many of us have stopped and asked: "What's next for me?" "What am I supposed to do with my life?" "If I choose this major or career am I going to succeed?" "I've really screwed up this time, how am I ever going to turn this around?" What if you just don't know? Your life feels a little out of control. You have all these questions; you might be frustrated with certain situations in your life. I get it, we've all been there. For the record, overthinking doesn't usually create solutions. If anything, it will make you overthink about 10,000 other things along aside that one thing you were initially thinking about, and now it's 4 AM and you realize you haven't slept all night. Well buddy, you haven't slept because you've had your brain running at 100 M.P.H. during the time it's supposed to be on autopilot . It's so important to know how much focus we need to give on the things that actually matter. Honestly, that's the interesting thing about life. It's like the Discovery Channel: you end up learning all these cool things no one ever warned you about.

Where do I begin?

It all starts with you. You have all the pieces to the missing puzzle. You just have to stop whatever you are doing, relax, and listen to yourself. You have the answer for what your next move will be, whether that's in your career, relationships, or any other situation.

We live in a very fast-paced, sometimes ego driven, and at times a very confusing world. I'm sure you've gotten the 20 year-old syndrome. How do you know if you've been infected by it? Well, one day out of the blue you wake up feeling more lost than your dad going through his mid-life crisis and convincing himself he needs the latest Harley-Davidson motorcycle. You may not even know what you want, or who you really are. Maybe you grew up Catholic, but now you question if there is a higher power at all. You'll pretty much question everything. Know that it's all good, just about all twenty-somethings have gone through this phase. Hell, thirty and forty and even sixty-somethings have experienced it. Well, I have some good news—this is where the fun begins. This is where the self-discovery starts. You've just gotta relax—sounds counter-productive, right?

Scattered brain, just chill

First and foremost, take a very deep breath and disconnect from the world. Detach yourself from the ideas and standards of society and those closest to you and ask yourself a few questions. If you are discontent, or more lost than your mom trying to understand modern humor, just ask yourself:

"What kind of life would I actually like to live?"

"How would I like to feel?"

"What kind of career do I want?"

"What kind of relationships would I like to have in my life?"

"What type of person do I want to become?"

During your moments of interrogation, be still and

fully honest. Do the things that are true to you. Don't do things just because your current girlfriend or boyfriend or parents or whoever else tells you to. At the end of it all, do the things that will bring you joy in the long haul. I'm talking about that substantial happiness. I don't want you to go home and say "Well, this book told me to only do things that make me happy." You decide to devour a pint of caramel-covered chocolate ice cream. That is short term happiness, because I'm sure at the end of it you'll probably feel disgusted, sprung off sugar, and filled with a monumental amount of regret.

I hear voices

Shut the world out. I mean that literally: we've all got voices, and it's time to turn them off. Maybe it's the voice that's saying you are going to fail miserably, you aren't wealthy enough, you are too fat or you aren't smart enough. I'm pretty sure at some point we've had some of these unpleasant statements running rampant in our heads.

It might have gotten so stuck in our heads because

someone we care about said it at some point. I have some

really exciting news: anytime someone tries to define you as

inadequate they are absolutely wrong. Whenever anyone

tells you that you are less than or that you can't reach for

the stars, turn around, jump up and grab the stars AND the

moon. Remember that no one can tell you who you are or

limit your potential. Silence those voices, and start defining

yourself. When you define the essence of who you are and

how much power you hold, then you will be able to take full

control of your life. At that crucial moment those voices will

no longer exist and only yours will remain, the one that

actually matters.

Miniature changes

Living in the moment is the best way to live, and the only way to live happily. In my mid-20s I was told "change is inevitable." I never really put much thought into it until circumstances forced me to understand the concept. Things in life aren't guaranteed to remain the same. Things will always change in your life, and the easiest way to adapt is to embrace that change. Let me tell you some things that may change in your life—your income; the person who told you they would love you for the rest of your life; the best friend who once kept all your deepest darkest secrets; the parents who change how they treat you because they weren't supportive of something you did. You know what? They are allowed to do that. They are free to do what they want and so are you. Embrace that change as part of the journey.

How we react to change is what really makes a difference. Why is it so important to enjoy the present moment and not cling to the people, situations, and things we've fostered an attachment to? Because chances are things will change. Life is a cycle. Reflect back on your life. How many things have changed? How many things have you asked not to change? The more you cling on to things the way they used to be the harder things will be for you. It's like when people say "The generation right now isn't like the generation 20 years ago, they are exposed to so much more." Well you're damn right we aren't the same. Nowadays we have the internet and social media and guess what? Twenty years from now there will be an even faster-paced generation.

You have to be able to adapt. You have to understand that there is an art to adapting with the world where you can be an individual in your own right. It all boils down to how you utilize the different things we are being exposed to. Are you using it for good or bad? Do you know what people have been able to do with the proper use of the Internet and social media? They've built businesses with more flexibility. Hell, they've built new markets like ecommerce. On the other hand, there are people who utilize it with bad intentions.

Now let's bring it back to the smaller things that occur in your life that you have no control over. You have to move with it in the correct manner, because 99% of your life will change.   I used to believe that once someone told you they loved you forever, it literally meant forever. No way! People are allowed to be free, move how they want to, and change their mind and feelings, if that's their prerogative.

Embrace this truth: this is the only real moment. You reading these words in this book are real. What happened five minutes ago is no longer tangible and you can never recreate that moment. Be mindful that worrying about an hour ahead or even five minutes forward is pointless because we aren't sure how it's going to manifest, or if it's even going to occur, so just allow it take its course.

OH BOY!

I recall talking to a close friend of mine. He was going for a job interview for one of the biggest positions in his career. The way he described it, this position would have opened doors, provided a higher salary, and raised his overall status. Well, this friend of mine went through a series of five interviews, including an interview with the vice president of the company. Every time he would be done with one interview he would be filled with anxiety about how he did and worry if he would get a call back. He would say "Oh man, I think I did ok, they seemed like they were engaged in what I was talking about." I heard all of his worries throughout each interview up until the final one waiting for a call.

As a friend, I wasn't going to allow him to drown in anxiety caused by senseless worrying. My suggestion to him was go into each interview giving it your absolute best, speaking about your credentials and about how you would be an asset. Tell them what sets you apart from the rest and how you will be an asset. Then the rest let of it fall into place. You can't control what happens once you leave that room. They get the final decision on who they want to hire for their company and to be on their team.

Now let me remind you that my friend did a great portion of worrying through this three-week process. A day after his final interview they emailed him, thanking him for his time and consideration but they had gone with a different candidate.

Now let's step back and take a look at this scenario. Would it have mattered if he worried throughout the whole process? Now that he didn't get the job, did all the worrying make any difference? The answer is a big NO! It didn't make any difference, except probably raising his heart rate. As far as my friend goes, he ended up landing a much bigger deal with a different company two months later.

I honestly believe just like my friend that many of us worry about things we have zero control of, that are of no importance or relevance. The bizarre thing is, in the grand scheme of things, many of our thoughts are running around with no direction. Our brains are like a hysterical kid lost in a store looking for their mother. Just pause and think about all the time you have wasted thinking about the what ifs: "What if he doesn't like me?" "What if I don't land the job?" "What if I failed the test?" Understand that many things that you worry about haven't happened and may never occur.

2 S's= solutions & strategies

Now if you are concerned about something, don't sit and worry. Instead, start developing strategizing, that way you are giving yourself solutions. After that let the pieces fall where they need to. Give yourself options instead of sitting and worrying about it. That's the problem with many of us. We just sit and worry without thinking about the solution. So please do yourself a favor—stop and utilize the 2 S's! Be present in this moment, because at this moment for all you know that thing that you are worried about will never occur in your lifetime. Remember this moment is the only moment that's real.

There is always a silver lining

At the very end of everything, there is always a silver lining. What might be detrimental to you at the moment won't even matter a year from now. Remember that in life, you might encounter some disappointments. It happens to the best of us—hell, it happens to all of us. My mom used to tell me there is a solution for everything except death. I know it sounds dark, right? My mom's wording when it came to life lessons tended to be dramatic and gloomy. I guess that was the only way her advice would saturate. So what does that mean? Anything that you are going through, have gone through, or will go through, there is a solution for it.

So you got fired from your job. Is it the only job? No, so immediately fix that resume up and start applying to others. You had a huge heartbreak. Maybe it made you fall into depression. If that's you and you're reading this book, get yourself up now and know that person was not meant for you. Good riddance to them. Rest assured that someone better is out there for you. From every downfall in life there is a lot of room to pull strength and victory from.

Inventory of time

During this period it's instrumental to understand life management. What is life management you ask? It's simple, it's just taking one step at a time. This is where you can practice your juggling skills that no one ever taught you. On your journey through adulthood there are so many things that you might need to manage in a span of a day. There is school, work, relationships, pets, and unnecessary drama that you somehow got webbed in. You will need to learn to prioritize what actually matters and structure your time well. We have a lot of time, and you spend your time on what has captured your attention and what matters to you the most.

The world has many distractions. Sometimes I watch people on social media for hours. Not intentionally, it's something I just notice by being around them. I see them looking at memes, making fun of someone who doesn't even know them, or just browsing senselessly. Then, that same person will look at me and tell me they don't have time to study, workout, or strive for their goals. I tell them "You are absolutely right, you have been on Snapchat so long that I would think you own shares of the company, but you don't, instead all you have left is a numb finger, and lost time."

I'm not saying to never indulge in social media or other extra activities you find pleasure in. I think it's great. What I am saying is be very mindful on how you are spending your time, especially when you feel like you don't have any. It all comes down to balance and priorities if there are certain things that you are wishing you did more of that would improve your life. Take a raw inventory of where your time is being spent and make edits. In the edit process you might have to make some hurtful cuts and extravagant additions. Trust me, it's not that complicated, we all have time, it's about how we prioritize it that makes a difference in the quality of our living.

The big H

Pay attention to your habits. We all have them, whether they are good or bad ones. Even from the way you step out of bed: do you place your right or left foot first? You may not even know, because it's something that you don't even have to think about you just do. Do something enough and it becomes a habit that you are no longer mindful of. Or, maybe you do notice it but it's so difficult to stop. I know for some of you, at one point, life revolved around partying and drinking from a keg on the weekends. Trust me, it can bring some interesting memories and hangovers. If you do it enough times it develops into a habit, and now you are wondering what year you started your drinking career.

Mindfulness of habits is really to help you not develop excess behaviors that overpower your good living. If there is something that you are doing that interferes with the many things you want to accomplish, then there is some reevaluating to do. Knowing your habits will allow you to know where you're spending time and what's preventing you from doing what you actually say you want to do.

Like many of us, you developed a "bad habit" and say you want to get rid of. It takes some time and a little effort, but be sure to replace that behavior with something else. Don't leave that space empty. We love our habits because they bring some sort of pleasure—we wouldn't do them otherwise. For some of us it's food, and I'm not talking about the good stuff like quinoa and spinach. What I'm really talking about is pizza, chicken nuggets, and your favorite ice cream. Instead of completely cutting everything out, which might lead you to withdrawals. Replace it with something that may also give you pleasure. Instead of ice cream try other, healthier options that will be fulfilling to you. Another option is to do something else entirely. When junk foods starts seducing you, opt instead for an activity that will move you away from those empty calories.

The other reason to be vigilant about the big H is because you will realize what you aren't doing. Like how about not meeting deadlines, or leaving things to the very last minute, or just really not completing them at all. You say this year will be your year, but you've said that since 2006 and now we're halfway through 2016. When I was in high school I used to always bring my schoolwork late, or just not do it. Then I'd beg my teacher to allow me make it up with extra credit work at the end of each term. Finally, a mentor of mine said: "These are patterns that you need to curve. You are becoming a procrastinator. You only feel as though you need to take action when there is a sense of urgency."

Well my mentor was right, that pattern continued years down the line. It followed me at schools, jobs, and life in general. I was so bad that I swear I was leading the band of the procrastinators. Becoming a procrastinator and turning that behavior into a habit will infiltrate just about every aspect in your life. It will overshadow who you really are. Some people may say you are flaky and unreliable, but that's not you—it's just the habits you've failed to replace. Just know that any habits you've created and want to discard, you truly can. It just takes strategy and patience, and at some point that habit will become second nature. Almost like when you jump out of bed, you don't even think about it and the new habit will take its place.

So the essence of being in the present, if you haven't before, opens the gateways of enjoying your life. Get real about the only honest voices you hear—the positive ones.

Understand that changes are actually much needed. You never want to be stagnant, so just embrace those changes. Those powerful two S's will subside your worries, because you will always have a Plan B in case things don't work out how you initially expected them to. It also allows you to reevaluate the way you are doing it. Keeping your habits and time in check will guide you to focus on the things that you want to grow in.

1ST GAME-CHANGER SUMMARIES

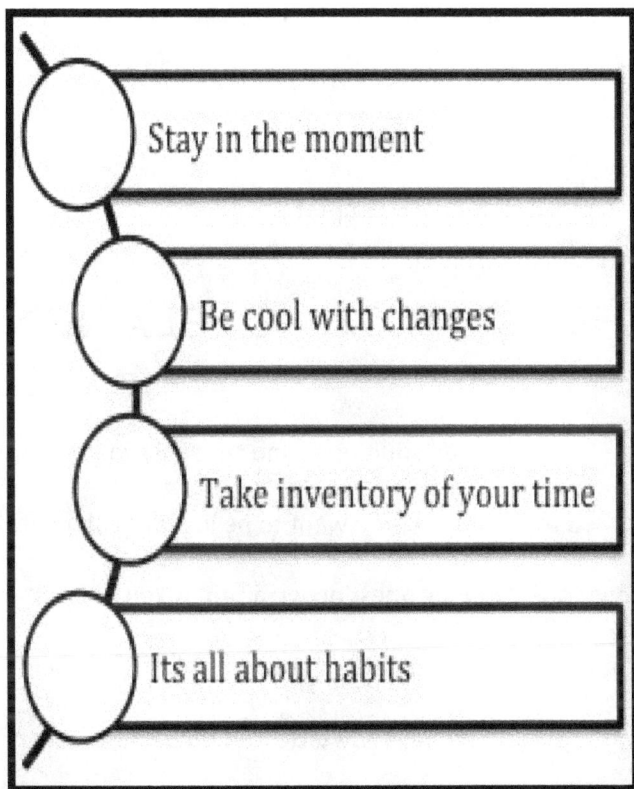

Stay in the moment

Be cool with changes

Take inventory of your time

Its all about habits

Chapter 2

THE ROAD OF REVELATION

So you are an adult now, and suddenly you're

supposed to know what you want to be in life? Yeah right! It

was that one daunting question we all got asked as kids:

"What do you want to be when you grow up?" Some kids

had their occupations already tatted on their chest. Other

kids were honest and shrugged their shoulders and followed

it up with a big "I don't know." Whatever the case is, fast-forward to now and after many attempts of trying to figure

it out, you are here asking for signs. You might be kicking

rocks and wondering what's next. I understand the

confusion stage. Trust and believe that it won't last long if

you are authentic with yourself.

Childish ways

There is this famous quote by well known author

Danielle Laporte: "Can you remember who you were before

the world told you who you should be?" Now what if there

weren't any limits that the world imposed on you? The only

imprint you will have in your mind is that you are

unstoppable, like you could do absolutely everything and

anything you want. Now many of us at some point have lost

who we truly wanted to be because society told us we

couldn't be that for whatever reasons. It might just be the

biggest perception we hold of ourselves, that we are

inadequate to be great. That could've persisted because

31

your parents told you the career you wanted to pursue wasn't going to make you any money. Probably the circumstances in your life have made you take a detour from what you actually wanted to do. Here is the good news: it's never too late to reevaluate your life and do whatever the fuck you want.

Do you know that's why you were chosen to be alive at this moment? There is something in you that the world needs—your talent, your voice, your generosity and authenticity. So take a long walk down Memory Lane and remember what you aspired to be. What did you do with ease? Whatever would make you content to wake up every single morning and do, do that. Listen to your inner voice, that positive one that's left after you've silenced the others. I'm sure if you refer back to it, it will bring you to a memory that actually inspired you to accomplish something fulfilling. Understand that there is no cookie cutter way to go about life. As long as you are striving to be the best version of yourself, constantly gaining knowledge, and ultimately doing what you love, then you're doing it right.

Action everyday momentum

Every single morning, take some time to envision what would make you ecstatic to wake up and do every day. I know I've been discussing vision a lot, because that's where it all begins, with that vivid imagination of yours, but it's important to follow it up with action. Many of us sit and envision this grandiose life we would like to live but then do zero to actually attain it. Your dreams aren't going to fall into your lap because you're sitting around wishing for them. You need to take action and always keep the momentum going.

First things first, list your skills—and don't say you don't have any, because you do. Do an inventory of yourself: what are you good at? We all have skills and strengths, so focus on those. Embrace what was given to you and work on polishing them every single day. If you write, don't just write today and then go on a year hiatus. This goes with whatever you are aspiring to do. Don't lose that momentum.

It's like trying to get in shape. You might start going to the gym, working out four times a week, and cutting out processed food. A couple of months pass and you are down fifteen pounds. You feel great. Then, you decide to take a whole week off from your new lifestyle. That week eventually turns into two and then a couple of months. Now you're looking at yourself like "What happened?" Not too long ago your health was a priority on your list. You gained the weight back and you feel sluggish and disappointed. Now you are screaming because you have to start all over again and you're wishing you'd never stopped. Well that my friend is what happens when we take time off on our goals. You lose track of time and go back to square one. So instead of taking breaks, make sure you are always feeding your dream. If not, you will continue to lose time trying to battle with it.

Now I am very aware that many of us may not have the luxury to spend all the time in the world to feed our goals. It's cool, I get it, but you need to make that time for it. I don't care if it's an hour a day. You might be working some retail job that you absolutely hate, because your boss is a prick and the customers are all jerks. The job pays the bills, so continue to work that job for the time being if that's your only source of income. But start taking steps in the direction you actually want to go. You might want to be an artist, an author or a painter or a photographer or whatever your little heart desires. Begin carving time out to dedicate to what you came here to do. Start dedicating that time to what you were brought into this world to actually deliver.

It can't be rookie season forever

Leaving prematurely isn't for the greats. How many of us are looking for the easy way out? To be quite frank, I've been looking for shortcuts since preschool, always trying to cheat the system. Finally a mentor of mine told me a couple of years ago that "anything worth having takes work." How many times have you heard that? Anytime someone tells you something worth having is super easy and it doesn't take much work they are straight lying to you. Any fast and easy gimmick is a joke. It takes consistent practice to have something great. How long does it take to get a PhD? The average student takes about 8.2 years.

At the current moment one of the dominant things in society is social media. Because of social media, I now look at the top media influencers in different ways. They are providing content nonstop for their fans to be entertained. Some are providing beauty, health, motivation, and educational tips. There's so many types of social media influencers, and the ones who are succeeding is because they are delivering content week after week nonstop. For some of them it takes years for them to reach the fan base they have, but the most known ones have never given up.

Now take that example and utilize it in anything in the world. You want to become an entrepreneur, know that it comes with hard work. You have to know the ins and outs of the industry you are in. Business can be very risky, just look at the statistics,but if you are always strategizing and working nonstop you won't have any time to even want to leave prematurely. Many people leave right when they are about to touch the finish line. Don't be like them. Keep pushing at what you want to have instead of giving up like a sucker. Many of us believe things are difficult, but get out of that mentality, because it will convince you that giving up is the right thing to do. So suck it up and keep pushing. If you want something, you have to stick it out. Stick it out until the end.

It's all about the risks baby

During this time know that you will have to take some risks in life. Be sure to make them calculated risks— that is, don't be afraid to leap as long as you see the landing. Many times we view risks as something negative when it's the opposite. There is a lot you can learn and ultimately grow from. People are always fascinated by those who have been bold and fearless about making moves in their lives. The cool thing about risk is that it shows you how courageous you really are. It pushes that confidences through you, so don't be afraid of risks. They will make your journey a lot more interesting.

The nation of labels

Let me warn you that our minds are wild creatures to be tamed. Your mind will challenge you, but take this as a fun game and start training your mind. Key word: YOUR; it's yours, it belongs to you, not the other way around. Just how we train for everything else, train your mind. It plays the most important function in your body. The old you might have said "I'm not skilled enough, I'm not worthy enough, rich enough, skinny enough, anything enough," but that's nothing but garbage. During this process it is imperative to be in the moment. As long as you allow those negative little thoughts to run rampant in your mind, you will be filled with self-doubt. If you give consent to them, those false statements will run loose and you will lose the battle with yourself. You must not lose to yourself—you are your biggest cheerleader, and you deserve greatness. As soon as those thoughts start flying, take a deep breath and tell yourself "I got this, I deserve success."

So remember that the power of labeling plays a big role in your search for eventual victory in your grandiose calling. Remember this tip: don't label yourself anything you wouldn't call someone you really love. Yeah I know, it's a cliché, but it's a fact. Have you ever heard that saying, "fake it 'til you make it?" Well, apply it to your life. I did this really cool exercise every single morning I listed fifty attributes and traits that I wanted to embody. Then, I repeated them every single morning and night. That took me in the direction I wanted: to celebrate who I am every single day. Don't want to do fifty? Then start your day with seven affirmations of who you are or who you want to be and say them over and over. You might struggle with self-esteem, doubt, and fear—many of us have at some point. But train yourself every single day to not embody any of those negative thoughts that will only cripple you.

A cool saying I enjoy repeating is "damn champ, no one can do it like you can," and then I follow it with my widest smile. I mean you have to have that über confidence, that is so astonishing it protrudes through your pores . That kind that gives you such a presence in the room that people just want to flock to you hoping that some of your dope vibes rub off on them. Time is something that we can't retract, so don't spend years bullying yourself. That's what I call it when I witness someone putting themselves down. Why would you be tough on yourself?

Some people spend years bullying themselves. I've been guilty of it. Be mindful that when you do say these negative comments about yourself, it doesn't fix anything. It only helps to drown you in those thoughts. Please take a lifesaver and swim your way back to shore anytime you even think of bullying yourself. Try this every time you are

41

ready to say something that is untrue and diminishing to your character: stop yourself and replace it with the opposite adjective three times. Train yourself to only say encouraging, positive, and kind words to yourself. You have to restructure your mind. It is yours and you have control over it, remember? Once you've trained your magnificent brain that you can actually accomplish what you want and become who you are meant to be, it will guide you all the way through your journey. Just believe in you, bet on you, it all begins with you.

Mastering Fear

Anytime you encounter the overbearing, hyperventilating, suffocating jerk named 'fear,' remember these words: "Fear is an illusion." It's all created in your mind. Remember that fear won't allow you to breathe. It keeps you stagnant from your great endeavors and future accomplishments. You have to become fear's opponent, and with that being said you have to know it in and out and how to beat it.

Welcome to Miami

I remember when I decided to move to Miami. My vision occurred after a trip with a few friends during spring break. I fell in love with the warm air, the culture, the colors in the sky, the aqua color of the beaches, all of it, really. Something about Miami just felt like home. I recall leaving Miami at the end of the trip and feeling heartbroken, like I was leaving home. It was something that I'd never felt before. I told myself before I left the sensational '305' that I was moving there. I knew that feeling was something I couldn't ignore. I tried to save as much money as I could. It wasn't much because at the time I was a broke twenty-something. I rounded up around 1500 dollars, tops.

Everything happened so fast. I told my immediate

family about two weeks prior to me making my move. Mind you I had already purchase my one-way ticket, found housing, and applied to close to thirty jobs. I choose not to have the conversation with anyone because in my heart of hearts I knew that I wanted to be in Miami. I wasn't going to allow anyone to tell me differently. I reassured myself: "I'll make it;" "I have skills;" "I'm educated, creative, and bold;" and those were the only thoughts that remained in my mind. So I left for my dreamland, just me, myself, and I.

The last thing that I was going to allow in between me and my dream city was the voice of fear, be it mine or someone else's. I went for it, I took the risk, I leveraged my skills, and I didn't sit and stew with fear. Instead I utilized fear as energy. I transformed fear into exciting energy to prepare as much as I could to move out of Boston and to my new home. When I tell this story, some people say "What if this would've happened, what if you didn't get a job, what if you got home sick, what if the transition was too difficult?" and any number of other fretful blurs of questions. None of these "what ifs" ever once occurred.

I've now been living happily in Miami for the past two years. Could you imagine if I would've allowed the illusion of fear to overcome my dream? What would I have missed out on? I'd be without that shining Miami sun, the vibrant energy, and the colors of the South Beach sky, unlike any other. I call it the "cotton candy sky," because when I see the sunset I can almost taste it. Don't ever allow fear to manipulate your life and your dreams. Face fear, punch it in the face, and utilize it to fuel you.

Adversity

Each experience you go through writes the pages to your stories. The best metaphor I can think of is your life is a jigsaw puzzle of 5000 pieces, and only when you place all these necessary pieces together will you be able to see the big image. Once you start to embark on the journey of finding your happiness will you start seeing the big picture. I refer back to my life and I tell myself, "Wow, if this situation wouldn't have occurred I wouldn't be here." Refer back to a situation in your life, one that happened a while ago that you've overcome. Now get a little closer and analyze the situation: if that wouldn't have happened, would you be where you are today? It's what makes up who you are. Don't be afraid to fail, and don't get webbed up with that word either.

Many people think that failure is a bad thing. It's not as detrimental as you think. You just dust yourself off, look for alternatives and try again. If you look back at the greats, they have all failed, but they've come back swinging even stronger. I look at failure as an extra layer of tough skin. It allows you to reevaluate and ultimately open yourself up to brand new opportunities.

Living in the city

I have a friend who was head over heels with her first love. They lived in this cozy apartment in Manhattan. For several years, she and her boyfriend were attempting to have a baby. At this time she was very young. Being young and in love will make you do things, beautiful, wild things you never thought you would do. They really tried hard to conceive, but she wasn't able to. Fast-forward to a year later, she discovered that her boyfriend was being unfaithful. On top of that, he impregnated the other woman. Since then, she has that turned it all around. She asserted her independence and took her life back by the horns. She enrolled into college, began traveling, and started to experience life in a new light. Miss Thing fully got her groove back. Most importantly, she appreciates that it wasn't her time to conceive for various reasons. Life was telling her that there was way better in store for her.

This is what life will do. A lot of the times it will tell you this is not your timing, and you must be flexible with your journey, because it's preparing you to walk through

other doors and shine through.

Kick ego to the curb

During your thriving years you will come face to face with this character called ego. We all have egos. We tend to craft our identities around our titles, we make judgments, and we cling to material possessions and status. Don't lose the sense of who you are because you are being driven by your ego. Society wants you to believe that you are great because of all the degrees you have attained, or the designer clothes you wear, and all sorts of other meaningless bullshit. The true essence of who you are has nothing to do with anything you've attained. Granted, we strive for what we want to be in the world, but we are more than that. You need to grasp the fact that when we strive for greatness it is not to look down on others but to give back to the world. That's the entire purpose on becoming a better version of yourself. The moment you start judging, belittling others, or identifying yourself by the things you have, you've lost both the big picture and real happiness.

We are flooded with all types of media in this era. Don't make the mistake of comparing yourself to others. Some people spend hours looking at what others have, what they are driving, and what's the latest exotic vacation they've taken. It hardly matters if it's factual, just that they saw a few pictures on Instagram. Whether they have or they haven't, understand this: it's not your life. Don't spend hours on virtually living the lives of others. Do yourself a favor—get off social media if you are on there to judge and compare, and start living your real life.

2ND GAME-CHANGER SUMMARIES

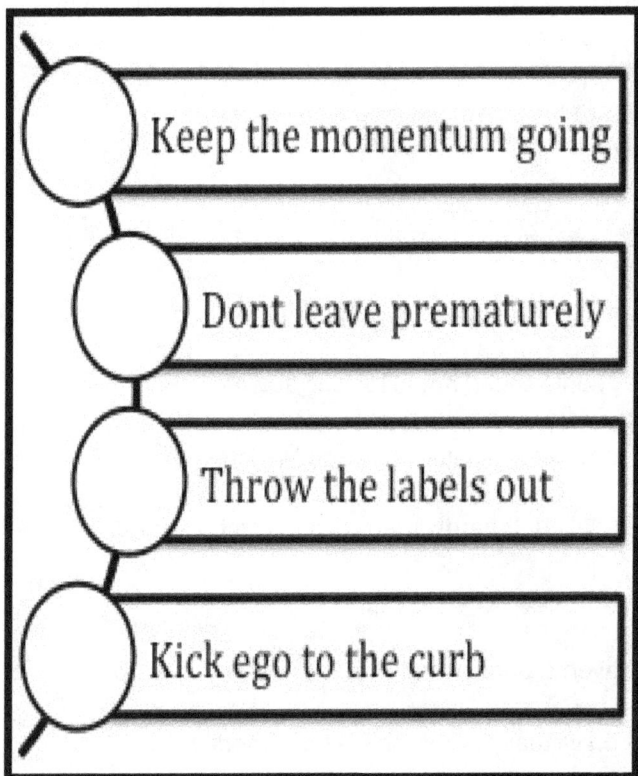

Keep the momentum going

Dont leave prematurely

Throw the labels out

Kick ego to the curb

Chapter 3

SERIOUSLY MEAN IT

Step into your life and all of the things that you do

with intention. Don't half-ass your life, you are the only one

that gets to experience it 24/7. I'm pretty much challenging

you to be at 100 at all times, and if there are days that you

aren't really feeling it push through anyways. Be this active

in all aspects of your life—relationships, career, health,

finances—live it all with conviction. Wake up every morning

like it matters. Train yourself to view your life in that way and things will start shifting.

Understand that we are only stardust in this universe and that at any moment we can simply disappear into the vast galaxy. If you were to leave this next moment, is there a dent that you made on this earth? What's your mark? What is your legacy? Have you started paving a life that would be thrilling and inspiring to read? If you haven't, start that shit right now. Do you know what the odds of you being born are? Well they are 1 in 400 trillion. That's crazy right? With that being said make every minute count, because it does. Your life is valuable or you wouldn't be here trying to get a better understanding of how magnificent and unique your purpose is on this earth.

Think how you feed your life in all the major areas. Are you doing things with love? Are you going into your problems with a mind of pessimism? Or are you thinking "I love my life so much, I will change the circumstances." Think about problems in that regard, battle your issues with understanding, and think outside of the box so you can grow. I know when someone is in love and passionate about any areas of their life, and so can you.

I'll give you an easy one, Ask someone how their love life is. If they respond eh, it's cool, I'm dating here and there; women are difficult to figure out; men are dogs; etc. and so forth. Clearly that person hasn't perfected their love life or it's an area they are neglecting. Now ask a person who has been pouring love into their love life. You will notice the glow that person gets when talking about their significant other. Their tone of voice changes and the excitement lights up in their eyes, because love moves things. It changes people. Please make sure you are speaking love into all the areas of your life. If you have children speak love into them. Speak love about what your passions are. Speak love into your whole life and it will transform it.

The dirty grind

I'm sure there are many things that you want to occur in your life right now, and wouldn't it be awesome if we could have what we ask for immediately. We live in an era where we want that immediate gratification. For any current news, all we have to do is look down to our phones and in .01 second—*taddah*! We receive what we are searching for. Well wake up, honey-bunches-of-toast—chances are your dreams may not happen that rapidly. Here is a misstep that many people make during the process—they hate the process. Baby, you better start loving the whole excursion, the grind, the progress and the triumphs and the missteps. Love it all, because it builds the story to your success. Allow each step gradually, so that it will become the following chapter to your masterpiece, the one that no one can duplicate.

If you love writing, don't talk negatively about the process. Talk about how you pushed through, how the words came running to you and you tried to capture them all ever so gracefully. I know a lot of writers that talk so poorly of the process of writing. They put all of these negative vibes into their work. Be thoughtful with any project you immerse yourself in. I know sometimes it can get tough to be 100 with everything, but you know what life doesn't care. You better show up ready, full of good vibes and the spirit to push through no matter what. I just want you to realize that we only have one life, only one chance to live our dreams. You weren't meant to be here and live in mediocrity; you are meant to do extravagant things.

Try not to complain. I always tell people if you aren't doing anything to change the circumstances, then I don't want to hear your toddler cries about how life is so hard. If that's your perspective, if you really believe that, then guess what? Life is going to be hard, because you believed it into existence. Keep shifting your focus to what excites you and what actually matters.

Fuck your past

In your 20s, you will make what some people like to call "mistakes." I don't perceive them that way because we make our own choices for our own reasons during our lifetime. If you feel as though you could do better, then take the action to start changing your ways. You need to be able to take charge of reinventing yourself if you feel like there is improvement to be made. We all have some type of behaviors we've indulged in that, if we're being honest, we aren't proud of. Maybe you acted on them because at the time you just didn't know that it was wrong. That's fine, we are human. As long as you are learning from your past choices that's all that matters. It might take you twenty fails to finally stop doing that particular behavior, but as long as

you overcome it in your journey then that's OK. And if,
when you change those behaviors, you feel any lingering
guilt of the person you used to be, make peace with that
because that's no longer you. You are never your mistakes.

I use to have this joke that I need to repeat a
mistake several times just to make sure I'm not wrong.
Well, when I finally turned the corner, I would get some
people in my ear telling me "remember when you used to
be this way and act this way?" I always responded politely:
"I don't sit and reminisce about my past, and I don't think
you should either."

I believe that when you make mistakes some
people believe they have the authority to judge and criticize
you, but they are wrong. They haven't lived your life, so let
those comments roll off of you. The old you no longer
exists, and the new you is here to stay and develop. Who
you are at 20 won't be the same person you are at 29 so

don't allow yourself or others to judge you on your past.

Remember, it's your past, not anyone else's.

3RD GAME-CHANGER SUMMARIES

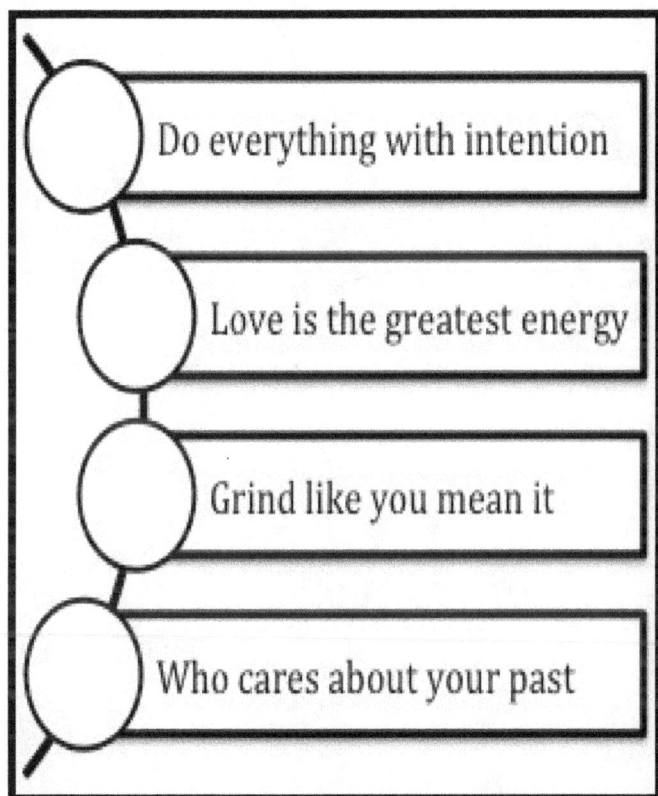

Do everything with intention

Love is the greatest energy

Grind like you mean it

Who cares about your past

Chapter 4

YOU CAN'T SIT WITH US

In life, it's important to know that relationships will be an important aspect of your life. You need to know how to be a good judge of character. Equally important is knowing how valuable it is to invest in those around you.

You have full authority of choosing the individuals in your life. You will learn who to keep on your lovely yacht that is your life. You will also learn that there are going to be some who you will need to direct to the exit, but that's the whole beauty of life. You learn and then you attempt to not do the same shit over again. I challenge you to embrace this concept. Your inner circle includes everyone that you spend ample of time with, even the people who you believe you owe some loyalty to. This includes family members, best friends, and whoever you may consider your homie. Now you must ask: "Why should I be so selective with the ones around me?"

First and foremost, you are whom you sit with. Just like in high school, I'm sure a teacher or parent told you that "birds of a feather flock together." Therefore, once you let go of the ones that are a downcast in your forecast, you will see how your life starts shifting and opening up to more grandiose experiences. Devote yourself to maintaining a great inner circle. Have people who support you, breathe greatness into your life, and are full of positivity. In the end it makes a huge difference. The people we choose to do life with are the people we cultivate our successes with. We are human beings and are influenced by those who we engage with on a consistent basis. This is inevitable. Look at the people you constantly have conversations with and the topics you discuss. If you and the other person didn't have the same values or beliefs in the grand scheme of things well then you guys wouldn't be partaking in the discussions.

Invest in the right relationships and they will be gold in your life. Make sure that you get mentors who you will influence your life and give you some direction. Know when to burn bridges and when to keep them sturdy. Spending time with those who play a positive role in your life at any capacity will deliver you nothing but greatness in your life. Know that we aren't here to do life on our own, and the more people who shed light on to your life the better it will enhance it.

Cut the hate

Gossip is for the lames. I mean, I get it, but we've been gossiping since we can remember, and the media perpetuates that by stalking celebrities' lives. The thing with gossip is it's not conducive to anything at all, plus you've lost time. You just sit around talking about someone for whatever your reason might be. I've witnessed people say they were just being funny at the expense of hurting others feeling by judging them. Even worse, the other person they spend time talking about doesn't even care or know them. Please question others' motives when they are bashing people, and question your own if you are doing it. It's never okay to spend your time tearing people down when you can be doing productive things for yourself.

I will give you the hard truth why some people gossip: that big dumb H. It's a habit. It takes away from focusing on themselves, their low-self esteem, their ego, or their ignorance. People who are out in the world making moves and putting positivity out there for others aren't gathered around talking about others' lives. Now, I will say that there are the media outlets who are gather around a table trash-talking. They chose that as a career and are getting paid to deliver gossip content. But, heads up—you don't work for them, nor do you own a share of the company, so cut the shit out. Instead of just sitting around gossiping about others, talk about new ideas or projects you are immersing yourself into, or what you are doing with your life.

A little understanding

In such a fast world it will be vital for you to come to grips with understanding others. We aren't all the same, we don't do things the same way, and that's OK. At times you will feel like people are wrong. The easiest way of you coming to grips with others is just taking the time to understand their 'why.' We all have a background for why we behave the way we do. For example, someone who is hostile and defensive might be suffering from a traumatic experience. Meanwhile, you've written them off as being a complete jerk. The reason why it's important to be understanding in life is because it will really help you in the long haul. Sometimes we are in spaces with people we can't see to see eye to eye with, be it at work, school, or even your friends and family. Understanding their 'whys' will release that block between you and them. It might not mean that you will be best buddies, but your approach will be a lot different.

The art of communication

The big C! Yes, it is vital in all relationships. Become friends with the big C. Embrace the big C at all times. When having relationships with others it's so important to express all of the important information that relates to both people.

You need to express if something is bothering you, but in the right manner. Sometimes we feel as though we don't want to have a conversation with others because it could come off as "confrontational."

But that's not the case—you are an adult, and adults have conversations to enhance relationships. It's just packing down the art no matter what the topic is. Be aware of your body language, tone, and be sure not to be dismissive while having a conversation. Active listening is important. People know when you aren't listening to them, and they will be dismissive of you once they realize. Be positive when you speak. Don't be judgmental or close-minded. Instead, try to understand their point of view. Ask questions if you don't understand, and if you are delivering a message be concise and to the point. Sometimes people like to beat around the bush for a solid thirty minutes. No one has the time to play detective and, quite frankly, it can get a little irritating. Understand that sometimes you will have to agree to disagree and that's OK. We don't always have to come to a consensus. Remember that we aren't all the same when it comes to how we think or perceive situations.

You + the world

In our era, the way we communicate with one another has drastically changed. Nowadays we communicate behind our laptop screens and keyboards and most definitely behind our phones. Because we are in this amazing, über fast era, we need to be cautious that we don't lose the sense of connecting with one another. Because we are social beings, we do have to interact with peers, friends, and whoever is in your surroundings, so losing practice will make it more difficult. There are many times when you actually have to face a human being in the flesh. You will need to engage in verbal conversations. You'll need solid body language. What I'm saying is you have to get out there, and you'll have to get comfortable in your skin to do so. For God's sakes, you live in it, so get very comfy with it and with the words that come dancing out of your mouth. The importance of being social is that the world's population is estimated at 7 billion people, and guess what? You, my friend, will have to interact with a few of them, so you might as well make this as smooth as possible.

You belong even when you don't feel like you do. Learn who you are. Learn everything about yourself, since you're the one who has to sleep with yourself at night. Know that there is magic about you and embrace it. People love seeing others who are authentic with others and comfortable in their own skin. Be open to be part of different conversations, and to be open to different perspectives. Take control and raise your standards. Be like that bouncer at the club. He pretty much dictates people's destinies for the night. Implement that same model on who gets access into your intimate life.

Begin to distance yourself from people or situations that are holding you back or draining you. Become aware of the energy and the environment you are in. Develop boundaries, as they're what keeps you safe. The first indicator of whether or not someone deserves a seat in your yacht: how do you feel around them? Do you feel uneasy, drained, or unmotivated? Pretty much any uncomfortable negative feeling that they are weighing you down with is a no-go. This isn't limited to when you first meet someone. Think about it periodically. Employers do it to their employees regularly. They evaluate their staff to see where they need to implement development and when they have to let them go. Friends aren't employees, but they should be a positive force in your life.

That's how everyone should be evaluated in your life—how is the individual helping you grow? How are you a benefit to them? How do they express themselves about others, their endeavors, and especially about you? You end up becoming the people you most hang out with, it's true. Your ideas become cohesive, and if that wasn't the truth, then you guys really would be staring each other blank in the face.

Expert advice

Start evaluating who you take advice from. We believe because someone is dear to us we must take their advice. But would you take legal advice from a mechanic? Absolutely not! At least, I would hope not, so don't start taking advice from someone who hasn't mastered the aspect in their life that you have questions about. For a very long time I would take love advice from individuals who didn't have the credentials to give them to me. These individuals would tell me to be careful, don't fully trust,

keep your guard up. So that was the mentality I took into

relationships. Could you imagine the baggage I brought into

these relationships. I attracted all those things, and when

situations would occur I would say "so and so was right."

But I started really dissecting my views and my thoughts.

Since I entered relationships with a lot of fear, I pretty much

did everything in my power to sabotage them.

Finally, I realized I should be dissecting the people

who I was taking advice from. I said: "Wait, what has been

their experience in that department?" "Have they had any

success?" And sadly to say, even though I believe they are

awesome human beings, they really didn't have much

expertise or had very negative views in that department.

Moving forward, I kept my love affairs and questions to

someone who actually was in a thriving committed

relationship. I listened to the ones who have experience and are succeeding in that department. When I wanted to enhance a certain department in my life, I would talk to those who had been at it for some time and could actually back up what they were saying with experience. So that has been a monumental lesson for me, and it has changed my life tremendously. It will change yours too.

Not everyone needs to know your next idea

I recall when I began discussing writing this book, certain people were like "What? Why? You've never written a book! What are you going to write about?" These were people who were very dear to me. Then I started talking to people who had experience writing books and have taken those big steps. They were more supportive: "That's awesome! These are the steps that I took and resources that might be helpful." Two very different conversations, right? They weren't wrong for not believing, but how can someone whose reality isn't yours, or who hasn't had any experience in what you are trying to do, even imagine what you are envisioning? Now the second group who I mentioned, has actually gone through the process of writing a book, so of course their response is "Definitely do it, go! Do it at 200 M.P.H!"

Not to say that the first group of people were bad, just that they couldn't see my vision. In their minds, it didn't exist. Now let me not throw everyone under the bus. There was a third group of people who actually encouraged me and believed in me despite their lack of experience. They were excited for me. I call them my cheerleaders, and we all need some. If you don't have any, keep continuing to be great and developing yourself. Soon enough, you will have cheerleaders on board who encourage your growth and dreams. Know that in this stage you might have huge ideas and it might be difficult to understand. That's OK, power through anyways. Know that there is certain important information that doesn't need to be shared with everyone. Share it with the ones who will support and encourage you.

Royal treatment

You know that golden rule that we've heard since like 1st grade? "Treat others the way you want to be treated." Well ladies and gents, it's very true. Be good to others. Treat them with respect and courtesy. Be a light to them. It's good to be a good person in this world, it's that simple. Plus, the world has this magical way of working in that it will deliver goodness to you as long as you genuinely spread it. Always be kind to others, even when things aren't looking so sunny. At times, we don't even realize that we might be causing harm to others. Whether we are going through a stressful time, or we haven't properly healed from prior situations, sometimes we are hurtful by accident. Now, you might need to check yourself, and if you are walking around irritating and being a ball of pessimism, then you need to take some time for yourself and figure out

what's going on. We are here to bring excitement, laughter,

and pleasure, so bring all the good to others. I'm telling you

that stuff is infectious.

Deserve it all

You deserve to be treated by others with respect,

honesty, and dignity. You deserve the royal treatment—

don't lower your standards to take the crumbs. You are not

some hungry lost bird. As you continue to develop in your

20s, you will realize how vital relationships are, and how we

aren't here to do this on our own, and how you need a solid

team. You will learn to master the skills of having and

evaluating relationships, and how to be great at them. You

can be an effective communicator. You can be supportive.

You can be that positive energy in others' lives. We need

more people like you, and you need more people who give

you that. Remember that relationships are like ping-pong—

you need two players to play well so the ball doesn't keep

rolling on the other side of the room.

4ᴛʜ GAME-CHANGER SUMMARIES

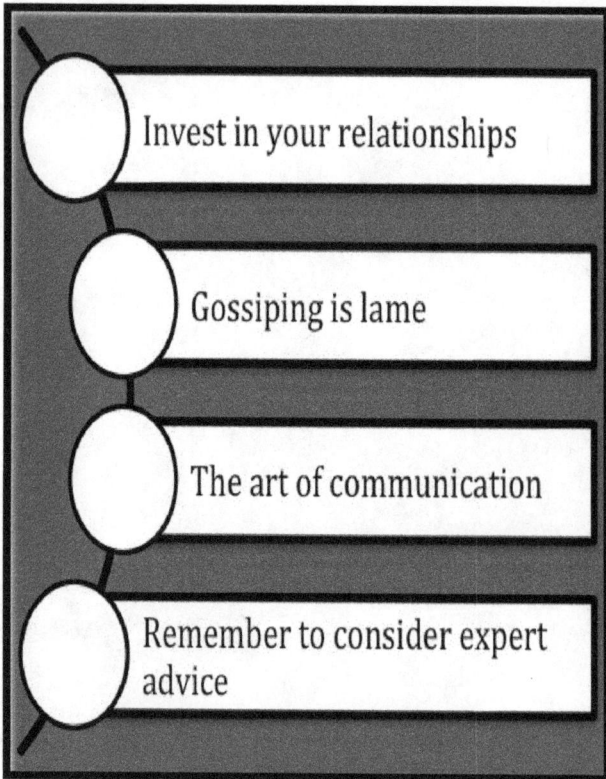

Invest in your relationships

Gossiping is lame

The art of communication

Remember to consider expert advice

Chapter 5

KEY TO BEING A SMART ASS

Do you know how valuable it is to educate yourself?
I'm not necessarily speaking of obtaining all those fancy
degrees, but if that's your prerogative then please kindly do
so. What I'm talking about is educating yourself in the
subjects that aren't taught in school. Educate yourself in
health, finances, relationships, and self-development. Why
is this important?

School in session

Many of the things that we need to know in life we aren't taught in school. Our school systems weren't designed to teach us the importance of finance, what healthy relationships look like, or what it means to value ourselves. Hell, what ingredients are actually in processed foods? High school chemistry tends to skim over that. Sure, school teaches you how to read and write. Hopefully it assists you in your path to discovering what you want to do with your life, but there are so many other things that matter that no one taught us. I am still waiting for the day that I will utilize all the algebra equations that I learned in the 9th grade. I'm sure mathematicians are grateful for all the algebra, geometry, and calculus they were exposed to, but for the rest of us who never figured out another variable, we question why we weren't taught more functional things in life.

How do you do taxes? Why are they important? Budgeting or investing courses would've made a lot more sense and it would've been very useful for many of us to implement in adulthood. Do yourself a favor and become financially literate because ultimately that's what you need to survive. Short of having someone willingly support you for the rest of your life, it's essential, and even then you should still educate yourself. Knowledge is power.

One of my favorite quotes from the great Warren Buffett is: "If you buy things you don't need soon you will sell things you need." That quote tends to keep me on my toes when I begin to consider making any frivolous purchases. I understand we can all fall for the temptations of marketing. Take a look at some of the items you purchase. You would be surprised how much marketing and advertising is makes them seem like shit you need and can't possibly live without.

Emergency funds

In your 20s, you will need to fall in love with the concept of saving. As habits go, this is a great one. I'm sure you are saying something like "But I'm broke! How do I save?" Save five dollars if that's all you can do right now, and start adding more to it each time. Set a goal for yourself. Make a budget. Write down all your expenses and look at what you need to spend and what you need to make some cuts on. A lot of the time we are spending on things we don't need. Cut those things out and don't live beyond your means. One time someone told me they needed $150 worth of cable, even though each month they were hitting overdraft fees with their bank. I reiterated an important concept to this individual that was to understand your needs vs. your wants. Moving forward, some experts say you need to save 1000 dollars for emergencies like illness, job loss, or car repairs. Others say you should have between three to six months worth of your expenses saved. If you aren't close to any of those two, you need to start saving.

First class credit club

To be able to do things like get a mortgage, get a loan for a car, or rent an apartment, you need credit. If you don't have good credit, some people will look at you like a freak. A good credit score, experts say, is around 720. You don't need multiple credit cards to build credit, just one is sufficient. Don't spend over thirty percent of the available credit each month. So if you have a credit card for 1000 dollars, only spend 300 of it, and if you do spend more than that, just make sure that you are bringing your balance down to the thirty percent mark. Understand that my synopsis on credit is very brief, but I cannot stress to you the major impact it will play in adulthood.

You are your best investment

A major game changer to thriving in your 20s is investing in yourself. Start right now. If you feel as though the four year higher education will further your career, then invest in your education. If you are an artist or an entrepreneur, saturate yourself in your craft, go in-depth with what you plan to do for a living. Know the ins and outs, and I mean really go hard and know your shit, and practice and put in the time. Go to conferences or seminars, read books, read articles, and listen to podcasts. There are numerous ways for you to find information about whatever your field may be, and once you do soak all that information in, apply it to your craft. That is investing in yourself because eventually it all pays off. The more you know and the more you practice, the more you will see results. I'm sure you've heard of the saying, "practice makes perfect," well let me tell you something, that shit is true. I've never witnessed someone who continued to practice and put in the time get worse at their craft. Have you? No, I didn't think so. Just thinking about the various things you have learned, the more you kept practicing at it the better you got. We don't know it all but what makes a difference is the practice we put in.

Health is wealth

I'm sure you've heard that the healthier you are the longer you live and the better you look and feel. That's cool and all because we all want that. Having really good health and taking care of your body now is the best thing you can do. Your body will thank you years down the line. Don't get sucked into the notion that you have to chug beers and take shots of tequila every weekend. Nor should you follow it up with pizza and french-fries. Having poor eating habits will lead you to spend more money, the money that you are trying to save and invest in your needs.

There are numerous benefits of taking care of the physical part of you. Exercising reduces depression, it boosts your creativity, and it reduces stress and anxiety. Instead of reaching for a temporary release, go and be active. Sweat it off. Knowing the right foods to eat is also important, so educate yourself about that as well.

The educational component of your well-being is really to focus you on the four areas of well-being, which are finances, health, personal development, and knowledge in your field. Be mindful that all of this goes hand in hand.

5ᵀᴴ Game-Changer Summaries

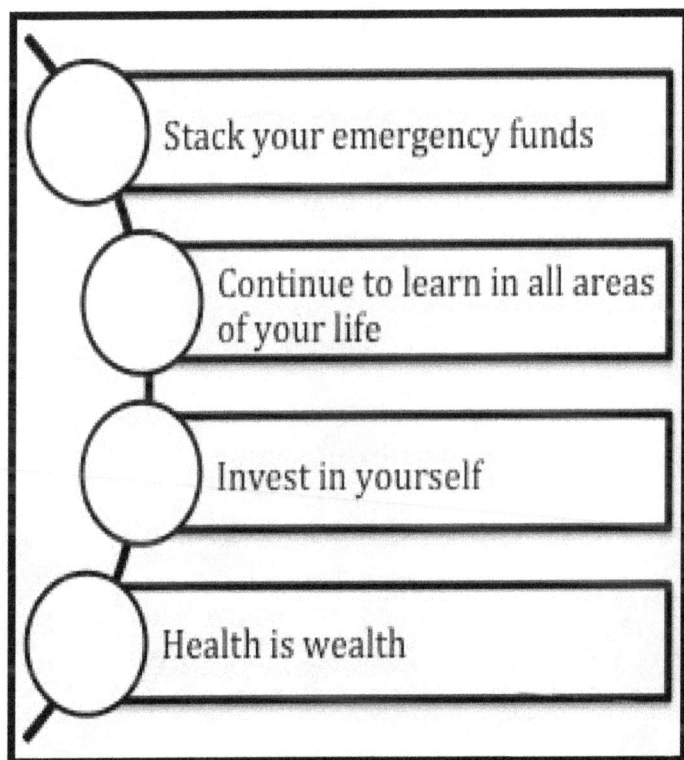

- Stack your emergency funds
- Continue to learn in all areas of your life
- Invest in yourself
- Health is wealth

Chapter 6

THE BIG YES!

You will come to realize that your 20s are your years

to "rock out with your socks out." These years are just so

crucial to your development of the individual you are going

to become. There is a lot of figuring out who you are and

you are going to be given plenty of life lessons, even when

you don't want them. These are the moments to completely

immerse yourself in all of the amazing experiences life has to offer. That is what your 20s are all about, you finding your path and finding out who the fuck you are. Do you know who you are? This is the cool thing about this stage, each year if you open yourself up to new experiences, you grow and evolve. You will figure out your likes and dislikes and what your strengths are. The more you open yourself up to the new and unknown the happier you will become. Your memories will be richer and your decision-making will be better.

Trust me when I tell you this, you don't want to be that person that regrets on not living it up. I know people in their 30s, 40s, and 50s wishing they were ballsy enough to travel more, to study abroad, or to be more social. I always encourage them that it's never too late to do any of those things. It just might be a tad different in that stage of your life, but it is doable. Remember, you can't relive the stage you are in any more than if you look back you can relive the years that have already passed. Today is the youngest you will ever be in your lifetime, so say yes to the new and the unknown—it just might change your life.

You might as well jump from a plane

Be bold and live—if you have a fear about anything make sure you make it a mission to overcome it. I remember when I was a kid my mother would take my sister and I to amusement parks. For any other kid in the United States, speedy, thrilling, and astronomical rollercoasters would fill a day with excitement, but for me was a day filled with several panic and anxiety attacks. When I tell you I was petrified, I mean I would cry my lungs and heart and pretty much any organ in my body out. My cries were the kind where you're trying to catch your breath and snot and tears are smeared all over your face. Finally, my mom got to the point of not taking me to amusement parks—I assumed she got the hint that I wasn't a fan of heights.

Years passed by and here I was, still afraid of heights, until one day I was like "This is stupid, I've been through a lot more intimidating things in my life, and my fear isn't even real. It's only real in my mind." I came up with my master plan in less than 30 seconds. Ultimately my plan was super simple. I was going to force myself to get on as many rollercoasters as I could until my fear diminished. I wanted to kick this fear more than anything. I began going to amusement parks, and each ride got easier as I worked through them, bigger and faster roller coasters, until it became exciting and the fear subsided.

I turned my fear into exhilaration. I had kicked my fear so far to the curb that for my 25th birthday my friend Andy and I decided to jump out of a moving plane. When I tell you that skydiving was one of the most liberating experiences, I couldn't mean it more. It was exciting and intense all wrapped up in a peaceful five minutes of overlooking the trees of Lebanon, Maine, on a pleasant day in September. Moral of the story is that me saying yes to life and coming head to head with my fear let me gain a lot more. I apply this method to anything that may spook me or prevent me from living my life to the fullest. I challenge you to implement this method to the illusions (fears) you might have created in your mind.

Explore beyond your fifty-mile radius

If you have the opportunity to travel to new cities and countries then do it, and if you don't then make an opportunity to do so. It will be a major service to yourself by exposing yourself to new worlds. Why live a dull life when you can spice it up by traveling to other countries and discovering cultures?

If you have never been to New York City, make an attempt to stop by. In New York the air is different and the energy flows at 124 M.P.H. It's a big melting pot in a very small space. The city is congested with high skyscrapers and innovative minds. I can tell you that Boston and NYC are two completely different cities and they are only four hours apart. You would think they would share many things in common but no, they are completely different and that goes for every single city. There is a culture, a movement, and a culinary identity unique to each city. Expand all your senses in every sense of the word. You only have one life, so act as if someone set fire up under your ass and run until that fire of wanting to see the rest of the world was real.

Any new country or cities you travel to you will find new things about others and about yourself. Be willing to get up and move to where you want to, and do it all right now before the responsibilities pile down on you.

6ᵀᴴ GAME-CHANGER SUMMARIES

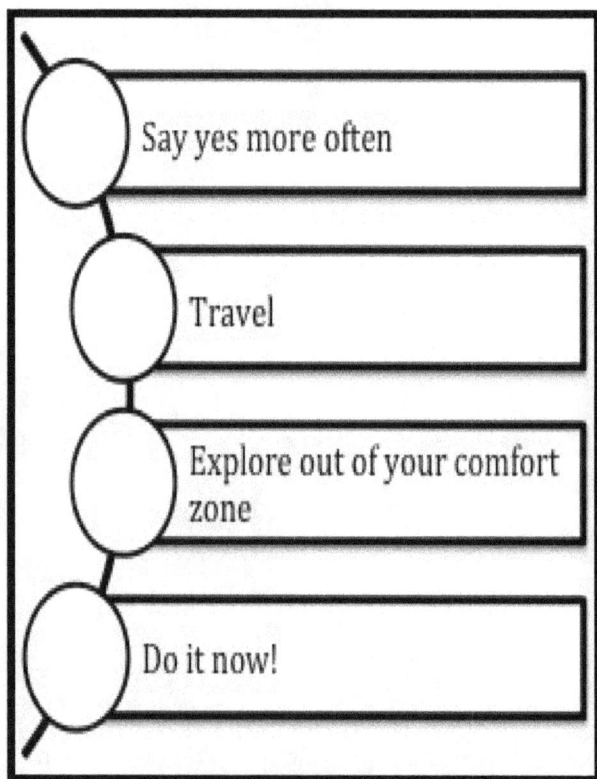

Say yes more often

Travel

Explore out of your comfort zone

Do it now!

Chapter 7

"THANK YOU" GOES A LONG WAY

Live your life with gratitude. Whether you had a

setback or a triumph or maybe you are you are just happy,

make it part of your routine. Wake up every morning saying

'thank you' for at least three things and another three

things right before you fall asleep. I don't care if your

girlfriend broke up with you or you just failed the biggest

exam in the world, being grateful doesn't give you room to be angry or to complain. It allows you to put your life in a different perspective. Word of advice—shit isn't that deep. I am going to tell you that the things that you complain about are stupid—very stupid. If you are complaining, chances are you are being ungrateful so zip it.

Crawling out of his skin

I mentor this young man from the inner city of Miami. When I first met this 15 year-old he would complain about pretty much everything in life, down to the color of the grass. I know, how can you complain about grass? God only knows. He would say that he hates that he lives in the 'hood,' and how his family is so 'ghetto,' how one time he had to live in a shelter with his mom and siblings, and how he goes to such a poor school. I can't blame him for some of the things that are frustrating in his life, some of his circumstances are bad, but I wasn't going to allow him to sit in his self-pity.

I stopped him and said "Are your expressions of disdain for your circumstances changing them? Thing is, this is your reality and you swimming around and drowning your mind in these thoughts makes you miserable. Start building a life in your mind that you would like to live. Because ideas and thoughts will start to take that direction, so begin to focus on your strengths. The more you focus on the positives and be grateful for what you do have, the more those things you want will be realized."

After some time he took my words into consideration and started focusing on what his strengths were. He began to write, to search for the greatness in his life, and he became happier. He realized that he had a lot of power in his life no matter his circumstances. He applied himself in school and extracurricular activities and his life started to evolve because his focus was no longer what he thought his reality was. He was thankful for his new perspective and for allowing himself to dream past his reality, because that gave him the motivation to move in the direction of his aspirations. He recently was accepted to a summer program at a prestigious university. His summer there is paid in full by grants from his hard efforts. You see, people fail to focus on the good they have in their life. No matter how bad things are they aren't that bad, and bad doesn't stay forever. Focus on and be grateful for the good in life and things will start moving. When you focus on the bad you become stagnant and sabotage your journey.

Shit happens for a reason

I will forever be grateful for my upbringing, even for the tough times. Let me tell you, it wasn't easy at times, but it has made me who I am. I have realized that it brought me to the right now, and I fucking love the right now. I grew up with a single mom whose first language was Spanish. She worked three jobs to provide for my sisters and me. There were times that we didn't see a tree for Christmas, and when heat was very limited if there was any at all. I saw her many times with such defeat in her eyes, but she kept moving on autopilot. At times her dedication to provide for us meant we had to raise ourselves.

But that brings me to now—I saw dedication, resilience, and a fight in my mother. It made me be so hardworking and ambitious. It also gave me a soft spot for the underprivileged population, the ones who are literally trying to make a dollar out of fifteen cents. It's given me a push to speak to our younger generation to be great no matter their circumstances, because bad moments aren't forever. Embrace the tough times because they make you strong, it makes you appreciative, and it molds you to do great in this world. I believe that it gives you that strong energy and fire within you.

The cool thing about appreciating the tough times is that it feels like a sense of accomplishment that you're no longer there anymore. I tell you that there is greatness to life. I look where my family stands now. We all grew up and moved out. My mother purchased a home in the suburbs of Boston and graduated college. She even started her own business. Christmas is a lot better these days. The times aren't sad because she isn't worried about bills, it's back to just enjoying good old' family time. I always wonder—would I have been so willing to give back and to reach out to the youth if I hadn't been through what I've been through? I don't know, but I do know that I empathize with others who have had life hit them over the head with a brick. I can relate to some of the kids that I mentor, and I'm able to motivate them and tell them that there is a much bigger world than what you see at the moment. All of this is bigger than you.

Pay it forward, without asking for anything in return

I've come to realize that serving others enhances your life. There is such a good feeling when you give to others and do something to change someone's day or life. Sometimes someone may need a word of encouragement. Some days, I think we all do. There are times where I've participated in giving back for a cause, and when I tell you that I got the most from just giving—giving my time, my words, money, clothes, food, pretty much anything—I do, so I will keep doing it. I know that we are here to give back, to plant seeds for the following generation and the generations ahead of them to create a better world. Use your power and gifts that you were given to enhance this world. I don't care if you don't have money, go mentor someone. Go to a food bank and give your time. Maybe that friend needed your encouragement to believe in them, or maybe it's that classmate or coworker that no one talks to.

Engage with them, say hello, be a light, you don't know what someone is going through. You could be someone's savior and you may have no idea.

Captain save-a-friend

I remember through college I worked at a retail company, and there was this girl who was very quiet and kept to herself. I befriended her because she seemed so mysterious from her silence and distant stares. She eventually confided in me and told me she and her boyfriend weren't getting along. He was very abusive towards her. She was only 18 at the time. I told her if she ever needed anything, that I'd be there for her. Well that one time came. She called me in tears and told me that she got into a physical fight with him and to please come and pick her up. I dropped what I was doing and drove to her house as quickly as I could.

When I got to the apartment, everything was turned upside down. Glass was broken, chairs were flipped—it looked like someone had raided this home. Then I saw my friend, fragile and heartbroken like someone had withdrawn the life out of her eyes. I told her "Let's go, where can I take you?" She asked to go back to her mom's house. I took her back and she left her boyfriend and everything behind. A few months passed and we fell out due to life getting in the way, but I bumped into her about a year ago. She said "I'm not sure if you ever knew how you changed my life that day, how you saved me. I couldn't cover the abuse anymore. If it wasn't for you, I'm not sure I'd be here. Thank you." I hugged her, and it reminded me of that day I saw her and held her.

The moral of this story is that you never know how impactful you are to someone by just caring. Moments like those are worth more than money, that feeling of gratitude

I felt just melted my heart. I looked above and said thank you, world, for being good. I tell you that the world pays you back. There have been crucial times in my life when someone has extended their hand and they have no idea what an impact they've made in my life. So be a light to others, we all need to be there for one another. You never know what kind of war someone is fighting behind closed doors.

The gift the keeps on giving

Whatever your purpose is in this world, keep giving it. Spread that all over town, the world, and the universe, just give it. It was given to you for a reason and for you to share. If you are a great writer, do that, and write and don't be afraid to show others your words on paper. Do you know how many times I've been inspired by others, their words, the tone that they use as they put it on paper? It moves me. If you are great as an artist than do that. I've met many people who are so great at a skill, and I'm like "Wow, I can see your gift in plain view, I can see so clearly what you are great at so you should do more of what you're here on earth to do." I sometimes see people say no to their dreams because they think they might not make money. Maybe others told them to take another path. Please do yourself a favor and do more of what you are great at and less of what you are not. Do more of what you love and less of what you don't, don't go wasting your time living a life that wasn't meant for you. Please spread what your greatness is all over this world, it will fulfill your life. Finally, be thankful for how far you've gotten and more will be given to you.

7ᵀᴴ Game-Changer Summaries

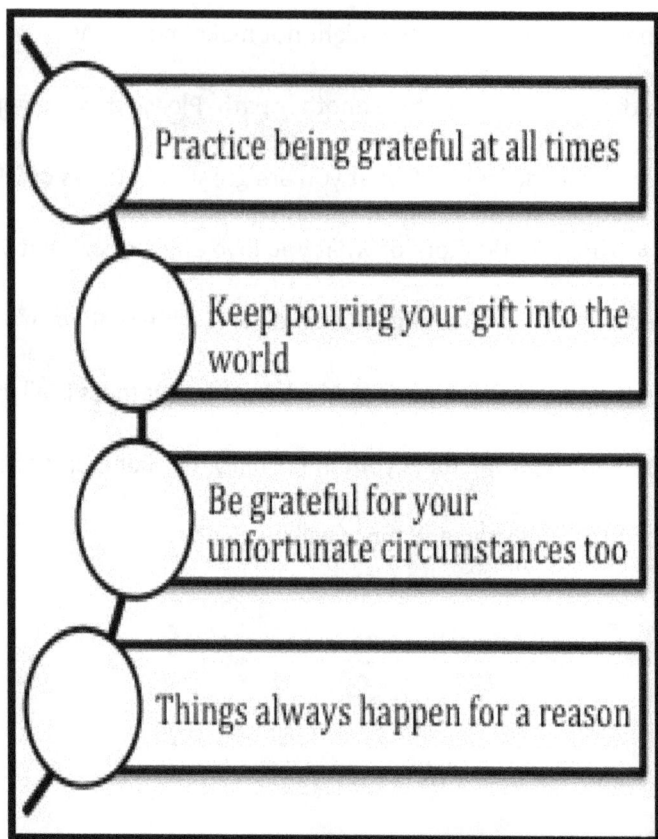

Practice being grateful at all times

Keep pouring your gift into the world

Be grateful for your unfortunate circumstances too

Things always happen for a reason

Acknowledgements

I have a bunch of amazing people to give thanks and acknowledgement to for the making of #thriving20s. I want to acknowledge all who have witnessed the making of this book for all of your support. Eileen Arugu, my first set of eyes on the first rough draft (and it sure was a very rough one), thank you for the true support and engaging feedback, as well as the design of the book. I want to thank my editor Andrew Daugherty for grasping my vision and all your hard work in thoroughly editing this bad boy.

I want to give huge thanks for all of the individuals who have played a role in my life. You have shaped my experiences in one way or another. I want to thank Adelita, mi abuelita, for always nurturing me with words of love and encouragement. I want to recognize my immediate family: my mother Beatriz, my second mom Lupe, and my two crazy loving sisters, Jojo, and Melissa. My dearest and closest friends who have always filled me with positivity and brought light to my life, Sarah, Ellie, Nicole, and the rest of my girlies. They say you leave the best for the last, so Jay, I am forever thankful for your motivating words, day in and day out, and your love throughout this whole process.

Author's Note

Well toodles!

I appreciate you so much for taking your valuable time and diving into #thriving20s.

Remember: everything is possible, and always embrace your greatness. It will lead you to extraordinary things. It is with much love that I created this book to inspire you and guide you through this cool decade of your, well, *thriving* twenties.

I want to hear from you so say what's up! Lets chat—tag me in some really cool, funky, chill, or weird photos of you and your new book #thriving20s.

Email: kfranco@k-franco.com